Small Words

SPECULATRIX

Chris McCabe was born in Liverpool in 1977. His three previous poetry collections are _The Hutton Inquiry, Zeppelins_ and _THE RESTRUCTURE_. He has recorded a CD with The Poetry Archive and was shortlisted for the 2014 Ted Hughes Award. His creative non-fiction book _In the Catacombs: A Summer Among the Dead Poets of West Norwood Cemetery_ was published in 2014. His work has been described by _The Guardian_ as 'an impressively inventive survey of English in the early 21ˢᵗ century.' He works as the Poetry Librarian at the Poetry Library and teaches for the Poetry School.

ALSO BY CHRIS MCCABE

POETRY

The Hutton Inquiry (Salt Publishing, 2005)
Zeppelins (Salt Publishing, 2008)
The Borrowed Notebook (Landfill, 2009)
THE RESTRUCTURE (Salt Publishing, 2012)

DRAMA

Shad Thames, Broken Wharf (Penned in the Margins, 2010)

NON-FICTION

In the Catacombs: A Summer Among the Dead Poets of West Norwood Cemetery (Penned in the Margins, 2014)

COLLABORATIONS

Gnomes with Tom Jenks (Red Ceilings Press, 2012)
The Debris Field with Simon Barraclough and Isobel Dixon (Sidekick Books, 2013)
Whitehall Jackals with Jeremy Reed (Nine Arches Press, 2013)
Pharmapoetica: a dispensary of poetry with Maria Vlotides (Pedestrian Publishing, 2013)

Speculatrix

Chris McCabe

Penned in the Margins

LONDON

PUBLISHED BY PENNED IN THE MARGINS
Toynbee Studios, 28 Commercial Street, London E1 6AB
www.pennedinthemargins.co.uk

First published 2014

Printed in the United Kingdom by Bell & Bain Ltd.

ISBN
978-1-908058-25-6

CONTENTS

ACKNOWLEDGEMENTS

Some of these poems were previously published in the magazines *Broadsheet*, *Poetry London*, *Poetry Review*, *Test Centre*, *Visual Verse* and *The Wolf*, and in the following anthologies: *The Best British Poetry 2013* (ed. Ahren Warner; Salt, 2013), *The Best British Poetry 2014* (ed. Mark Ford; Salt, 2014), *Gathered Here Today: celebrating Geraldine Monk at 60* (Knives Forks and Spoons, 2012), *In the Company of Ghosts: the poetics of the motorway* (ed. Edward Chell and Andrew Taylor, erbacce press, 2012) and *Double Bill* (ed. Andy Jackson, Red Squirrel Press, 2014).

'Teenage Riot' was written for an evening of poetry for Sonic Youth organised by Stinky Bear Press, and was inspired by the music of Louis Zukofsky's "A". Many of these poems were recorded for the Archive of the Now and are available as audio on their website.

Speculatrix

Speculatrix

Dedicated to Mark E. Smith, the last Jacobean

Black Lodge Recorder

after David Lynch's Twin Peaks

A black box is a device which has input & output mechanisms. Its internal workings are unknown. It is of the starling family & can often be heard saying "Leo, no!" Almost anything can be described as a black box, even the human mind. It is distinct for its wattled feet. The opposite of a black box is a snow warbler chirruping in porcelain. The death of a black box is often used in avant-garde TV dramas to set the tone for the series : ludic but chilling. Most black boxes now come pre-installed with Syrinx v.6. Although these devices are omnivores — eating mainly insects & fruit — their blood is redder than expected when it drips on an opened box of doughnuts. Humans, to pacify their lust for displayed intelligence, often attribute black boxes with names such as Waldo. Most species nest in holes so cages expose them to things they can't forget. "Leera, Leera; don't go there." Sometimes they repeat these things : "hurting me." Later models have developed extravagant facemasks as if it to remain anonymous. They have two eyes that turn clockwise to record & the voice licks itself strapped to black spools. Even when the black box is shot with a bullet its voice remains captured. "Stop it, stop it. Leo, no!" Although called a black box a black box is actually bright orange to make location easier after a disaster. The orange is the same colour as a mynah bird's beak.

spĕcŭlātrīx , īcis, f. speculor,
I. she that spies or watches, a (female) spy, watcher.

Charlton T. Lewis & Charles Short, *A Latin Dictionary* (Oxford: Clarendon Press, 1879)

Write thee up bawd, in St Paul's; have all thy tricks
Of coz'ning with a hollow coal, dust, scrapings,
Searching for things lost, with a sieve, and shears,
Erecting figures, in your rows of houses,
And taking in of shadows, with a glass*

* *glass*, a crystal or beryl ball which is supposedly
entered by angels which can be discerned and
understood by a *speculatrix*

New Mermaids edition of Ben Jonson, *The Alchemist* (London: A & C
Black, 1991)

The Revenger's Tragedy

In which Vindice speaks, avenging the death
of his betrothed Gloriana at the hands of
the Duke. The Duke is coaxed into kissing
the poisoned skull of Gloriana and dies.
We are here, Bankside, London, 1604.

I've seen skulls with better teeth than thís   excessive
    in death   as an eúnuch's archived *Playboys*
After the extraction the blàck sock in the ditch of the
mouth   a debit of bónes cindered in corsets as
Southwark's   abscess   drains   green   in   the
Thames   Just another *parched and juiceless luxur*
Bàck in the summerhouse I kissed a face once new, now
skulled núde   just to feel what absence was   a rat
blóated the one hole of light & now all authorship is
apocrypha, in the gross   scheme of things   I wear
these bónes in my mouth   when we kiss
    so you know how the gráve   plugs the mud with
the fillings of us   O Gloriana   *A bone-setter   one*
that sets bones together   counts for me the citrus pips

set in the black cement   men tossed overboard
     at The Cut   where white noise is a street cleaner
buffing an ambulance exhaust   I found a booklet
called EXTRACTIONS, it included your name & a
gauze swab   Here comes Death Dressed as Folly &
it's like the Reaper's fancydressed for the callcentre
    I have failed once again, I have no brother
SUPERVACUO, I have no brother AMBITIO.

Link me in the rain, where the cockroach of the cab
scratches its back with wipers   Link me because what
are teeth but calcified tíme plugged in pulp & dentíne
& gumlíne   The Glóbe on   Google Earth like a
shitbasin of rivets, a cistern of balconies   where the

pink skin waxes rootwards like a hymen returning
against the tíde of gravity   the cavity is just the ápex
before the acrid pestle   the crown of the tonguetip
          If you bótox my mouth then it's cáke & sàck
through the stent of a straw forever   & you dráin the
canal of me bàck to its source   where   the
heart in its dagger   invents   the   silence
                    where the tongue   in
midnight fíre   consúmes its purpose

The White Devil

Spoken by the Duke of Brachiano who visits the house of Camillo with the intention of seducing Camillo's wife, Vittoria Corombona. Vittoria allows Brachiano to visit her and she gives him a jewel; Camillo is killed by Brachiano's secretary, Flamineo, in what is staged to be a vaulting accident. Vittoria is put on trial for Camillo's death and sentenced to a 'house of convertities'. We are here, Clerkenwell, 1612.

Late nights around the eyes, cláws of blackbirds
    Woke three times to configure double negatives
Ersatz sleep, translúcent   In the dearth of winter
this audience has less wit than sparrows   Eros
Bállplayer whose side are you on?   You're no Bill
Shankly   Never share one madness with another
    it's subjective therapy & blood on your shoes
    Voyde out the earth & scatter our bones   Do it at
The Red Bull, Clerkenwell, where the hedge-funders
took our Players   séized our seats   we want back
what's rightfully ours   our concessions on tragedy
    Don't paint yourself whíte   it washes the rain like
London clay down gutters of mushed petticoats *we*
out-brav'd the stars with severall kind of lights   & if

there's a white devil there's a blàck star   drawing us
to the river's marshes   after houses   straining itself
into the Thames at Blackfriars   the zòmbiés of
ambition never come here   these hours belong to us
    when the pit has moshed us by syntax   when the
language we have paid for has made us sweat   & all
that is left is to make our bodies act out the desíres
they now have words for   images of us now
SUBTITLED in a way most moderne   Don't paint
yourself whíte until you're running whíte inside   in
the way the poet forewarns us   if you say you don't
want it, you want it   this is the double negative
of the flesh   which the brain in its maggot folds
idly watches   it has nothing to hatch

---

there is no choice

The Changeling

Spoken by Alsemero who has fallen in love
with Beatrice. As she is already betrothed to
Alonzo he gives up hope. De Flores, manservant
to her mother, also loves her. Isabella uses
De Flores to kill Alonzo, who presents her
with the ring finger of the corpse as evidence
and takes her chastity as payment. Now free
to marry Isabella, Alsemero wants to test her
virginity but Isabella swaps places with her
maidservant, Diaphanta, on her wedding night.
When Diaphanta doesn't come out from the
bedchamber Beatrice asks De Flores to start a
fire and then kill Diaphanta in the confusion.
Confronted, Beatrice confesses all to Alsemero.
We are here, unknown London location, 1624.

Out of The Cockpit, areólas of ash   riots run in cycles
   Drury Lane cleansed by midnight fíre   blue ribbons
of smoke over King William St whórled in your scent
   Exclam text from the bàck of a cab   pending the
morning's phrasesearch "exclam means"   the rúse of
Google so fucking literal   Did you mean: *"exclaim"*
   Here we are too soon for the dictionary   too late for
referral   that pending book just a system bereft of
thanatos   the rose anagram *éros*   Before the paradox
of   the   phoenix   a   conflagration   of   shàdows
& *brainsick patients*   mórph in the flames like red
cellopháne fish   if the heads & tails move   the
Fortune Paper says   we're both in love   The bricks
combust in reflexes   Beatrice your reflexes

combúst   the last trick of death, I read   fuck it's
attraction   this hoodwinked eíderdown of smóke
we come up for air in The Great Serotonin Comedown
of 1622   all we want is water & each other   The
buses   in   kindled   blocks   of   red
   we both have a smouldered city inside us   that is
the same   & though the Great Fíre is yet to come
      it will not alter us   my heart a splenetic fláme
   cindering ribs to crust   taking out the zòmbiés of
ambition   They will rebuild the same lines to walk
us down   these dead concocting dictionaries
         defining madness   We could have this
conversation at the door of any tavern   at any time
      but it's tonight   in this thirst   this first

---

combústion

A New Way to Pay Old Debts

Spoken by Alworth in rage against Overreach, an aspiring landowner. Alworth has fallen in love with Overreach's daugher Margaret, although Overreach is determined for his daughter to marry the noble Lord Lovell. We are here, Drury Lane, 1621.

Toenails blàck in the petty càsh   burnt pennies
        You cormorant   You catspaw   You cruel
extórtioner   beer & debt gnaw my endórphins
        You brach   You dogbolt   You hellhound
        beats & kicks him   ThIS IS THe ANNiversArY
of SELlINg YoUR SoUL TO H+t INsURAncE ApR
549%   This credit card you don't want has your
name on it   it can be couriered by Three Creditors
        You lean skull   You privy creature   You
sláve to meat   Fill this glass with whíte froth &
watch me knock it off   You   buyer   You drudge
        You ditch to what's inside   Enter "human skulls in
the Thames"   ERROR 404   You hedge-funders to
our best Players   You bond-slave   You cur

You son of incest   You cherrylipped mannequin of
blàck plots   After The George & the youth you saw
in my face   outside the Barclays where I signed my
name like a hair in whítebroth   *buttermilk cheeks*
     where I knew, at the Strand, there was no money
in poetry   but heard   in the truth of gráves
after drinkings, when you lodg'd upon the Bankside
there   is   NEVER   any   poetry   in   càsh

The Alchemist

Spoken by Lovewit who returns to the London he fled to escape the plague to find his home overrun with the ruses and deceptions of con artists Face, Subtle and Dol Common. Face wins a reprieve by stage-managing Lovewit's marriage with the woman he has fallen in love with, Dame Pliant. We are here, Blackfriars, 1610.

Will you be my speculatrix?   absence keeps us
guessing   this city can lick figs   I'll gum its silks
with cláy   *stuck full of black & melancholic worms*
    The old St Pauls was búrnt of trade & commerce
this hollow dóme's for confessions   blue was the life
motif for summer   & the youth you saw in my face
    London expells me twice weekly with plágue   the
provinces rehearse my art   like a coal stuffed with
diamonds the wax splits at Eúston   the zòmbiés of
ambition   march policies of truth   but poets are
liars, the wind whórls their value phones   I'm on
loan with words of àccént rísing   the terraces I've
come from   dictionary entries in duplicates
    definition FIRE licks my heels   Christ's blood in

carafes at business lunches   less toxic than sodium
glútamate   income enough to learn German   or go
back to therapy   Hoch Deutsch was not at Bábel   I
consort   with   the   small   poets   of   our   time
    the tooth fairy tweaks their nibs each night   & milk
leaks out each morning   When the bawd of Lambeth
meets the bard of Southwark   you get another
fucking Revenger's play   *This night, I'll change all, that
is metal, in thy house, to gold*   even the blàck fillings
in this skull   that are rocks around the skinned seal
of the tongue   if I show them when I laugh
that's   because   to   laugh   is   the   anti-death
    even against the city's new plágue   named
COMMUTE   There is no travelcard

to take us back   I have a real toy sword but am in the
wrong play   strung for a woman who circulates like
oil   whórled with rubber & roses
a *bonnibell*, the text said   a soft & buxom widow
      to this live skeleton   rattled with libido

The Knight of the Burning Pestle

Spoken by Jasper who is competing with
Humphrey for the hand of Luce, daughter of
the merchant Venturewell. Adventures in the
suburbs of North London. Venturewell thwarts
Luce's elopement with Jasper by forcing her
home, but Jasper fakes his own death and wins
Luce by gaining entrance inside a coffin. We
are here, unknown London location, 1607.

I'm in a Green Room, blood bóiled to aftershock   a
man in the calibre of redwood   a prefect with libido
        sweet-tooth incising for kudos   càsh in the
quarterpound bag, bonbons dry to the suck   based
mostly at 233 Eúston Road   I'm in a pláy with a
red toy sword   watching a play called *The London
Merchant*   What play are you watching?   These
travails of a mind led by desíre   would lead me over
Southwark water   for a quart of the house tap
        shared with you   Luce we've been here before
when our hearts were whíte   I have a squire & a
dwarf inside my mínd, when you compliment one the
other conspíres   the life motif for Summer   if this
should fail   it is for straining myself extraordinary

so laugh yourself to death   & meet me through stick
& stone in Essex   where the fox & kestrel made me
speak   a lexicon I didn't know I had in me   Words of
betróthal now lost to the marsh   I don't need them
bàck, I've got this graph of past emótions   The index
is scored in crow's feet   The youth you saw in my
fáce   erased   at least until the dark ales drunk at
minus three degrees   have sobered us to frost   & if
those we hurt won't pardon us   because this *plot of
our play runs contrary*   then *plot me no plots*
     Parting blankets the níght in snowy sheets   &
though we don't sleep alone   there is not the fíre of
waking together   If this can never be   this pláy is
speculatrix   a future portent

---

unbecoming in eternity

The Duchess of Malfi

Spoken by the Duchess who has secretly married her steward Antonio and prematurely given birth to his child. When the Pope intervenes Antonio flees, followed by The Duchess, but they are separated as Antonio has to leave for Milan with their son. Antonio is stabbed under mistaken identity. We are here, Blackfriars, 1614.

This is The Cut   the last act of drunkenness   *A deep pit of darknesse*   these actors rule Dramatis Personae   just two of us in the cast, Antonio   a neon rickshaw at Waterloo   In this gloomy world there are bars run by horses   midnight bookshops   our morals AWOL with dwarves   To be a lover in the winter   roots in our nerves   when all soil is dead   A red door in the Thames, the river its hinge   letterbox too lean for skulls to fit   when I lose my keys, will you let me through   to eternity   I'm in a red play with a real toy sword   you imagine my full attention   imagine me wanting you watching this   who's watching who? Speculatrix   *Now there's a rough-cast phrase to*

your plastique   The door opens a riverbed of dog's
teeth, bónes & trinkets   marriage transgressions for
non-privy punishment   Donne with the niece of a
Lock Keeper   imprisoned 1601   In the turn of Act
II we exchange a ríse for a kiss   this is how fucked
up this is   blood & florins across the balances   Only
once did we walk Lambeth in daylíght   our organs
turned to purple felt   Antonio, it was not the grínding
war of domestics   children watched us kiss   our
giddiness raged Vs business lunches   a combústion
with invisible cloaks   This question that grínds the
mind's pumice : why has time this death lease? it hurts
to ask   There are more reasons to watch a Duchesse
than to protect her from suitors   then keep to the

Majesty of wedlock, it keeps the devil in flesh
candies over all sins   with a coat of solace &
friendship   To play Intelligencer to your monster
        a beautiful monster   the devil's gentleman
        there is no difference between silence & lies
                when you're in the reeds, watching us
        The door will open its own red tíde   to a
heartshaped crab   that thinks sideways is right
                because it's what it does

Women Beware Women

Spoken by Leantio, a banker's clerk who has
married the beautiful and socially superior
Bianca. The Duke catches Bianca's eye and
instantly falls in love with her. Leantio,
broken by his wife's infidelity, takes a friend
of his mother's — Livia — as a lover. We
are here, unknown London location, 1621.

Your tears, Bianca, on a stage set as Florence   tubes
cascáde underground   Just two of us in the càst
    We lay down on dead soíl in February   in the
Priest's gardens   our hearts reverb the earth like
cellphónes   *Exeunt on a moonshine night*
LEANTIO   at   the   Holiday   Inn,   Southwark
    the whíte sheets of his excess stáins the autopsy
Do you think women love with reason?   Only when
they know horizons from beach level, the exhúmed
wharves you looked inside   frosted with verdigrís
    in the bladderwrack of the tide, a flake of Vísa, a
chunk of red door   Eliot's rat in my fingers, sliced
the length of snout & teeth   ceramic cenotaph
of this plágue that will only leave us   once it has

wormed our senses   *In stranger things there is no*
love at all, but what lust brings   then this love, in
Winter, for which lust búrns   for the cardamom of
Spring   We have *walked out whole nights together*
in discourses   our subjects are words, magic, gold
& ales   we trade what we've got in invisible fíres
                speaking in tongues & tonguing in languages
known only to us   in this combústion   our
senses are worms   Along the breakage of the
Thames, crowds upload their abacus of globes
        Your love damaged my life's little bird   this love
I need, Bianca, but cannot sustain   *So Many sun-*
piercing eyes   worming the senses   to see some
part of you tricked up toníght   my mouth in

alteration   &   although   we're   both   in   wit
we   are   as   cháins   to   this   circumstance
the   ones   who   can   help
the   helpless   ones

this world's end in both of us

The Malcontent

Spoken by Duke Altofront in disguise as malcontent Malevole, who feigns conspiracy in aiding Mendoza in murdering the Duke of Genoa and marrying Altofront's imprisoned wife, Maria. When woo'd by Mendoza, Maria defends her honour and marriage with Altofront. Altofront lays down his fool's disguise and is acclaimed as the rightful Duke. We are here, Bankside, 1603.

When passion overcomes the ordered vision of verse
Maria   our moral certainties break in próse   my
heart's in your fáce   inside a phoenix   rísing in
my chest   words of the New World   in Actus Primus
Scena Prima   our course is run   The orange was
a false God   it watched us think until it heard too
much   it had to go   the dry sinews like fabric
tóre through clouds   we tasted distant lands
     Lust cries for a surgeon   this madness our
therapist   On Waterloo Bridge in the midníght zóne
of March   I can smell the breath of my peers
tobacco & sodium glutamate   A mile &
420 years from here admit me to Middle Temple
expelled from chambers for non-payments & non-

residence   Maria   be with me when they
satirise us   for being bombastic in tímes of paradox
       If there's a War of the Theatres we'll keep the best
players   the rest are just boys   You wrote *purse* in
blàck across your hand   what would be in there?
       imagine the liquid gold running through your palm
This day is urban pastoral, a force that through green
próse drives these lines   *Purse* replaced on your hand
with *Debt*   indelibly writ   The smallest pub in this
world next to a gráveyard   that's where we'll go
          the tube reverbs like cellphónes beneath us
                    even when we're up in the balconies
You ask, Maria, what is this climax happening to us?
       to die once is to die multiple   John Marston

how could you do this to us?   We are metafucked
      This pláy we've writ ourselves in   when you were
ill   is ill-received by the small critics of our tíme
milk leaks from their nibs each níght   The feathers
we   wore   at   Blackfriars   blown   with   each   páge
                  our words too light for the gáles
    a price we cannot sustain   our livers in combústion
desíring hurtful drink ends both life & thirst   My
insults   are   stringent   it   hurts   you   most,
hurting   most   myself   *Shadow of a woman,*
what wouldst, weasel   If you bit me you would see
            the devil is my linguist   this tongue is
for keeps   *Three Demon Books* in a red bag splits
on London Bridge   if the river was to take them the

door would combúst   & though horn-mad we gave
no man horns   these *dumb and raw-aired nights*
                there were hotel shadows in our mínds
errors of wonder to strike dumb our senses   *We well*
prepared for change   We in force compelled to
silence   these words forever newly writ
each time your eye imprints   *How shall we waste this*
light?   whistling deaf foxes where the dock stains
the tídes?   Confessions at Blackfriars?
                Now   we're   in   Act   5
you know you murdered me best   when we first met
    when this was the right pláy still in commission
    when we met in the wings & you kissed
me   to   death   my   tangled   heart   like

ox-tongue, Maria   I have 10 attempts for the
password *éros*   before the application locks
          for our words, no backup   *cláws of*
blackbirds around the eyes   THE MONEY
SHOP courier asks for càsh in the bànk   Bank
Holiday revellers take it all for góld   a boy drops
sugar in the self-service box   & this love
becomes a honeycomb   The zòmbíes of ambition
struck dumb by the show   a structure well presented
& preserved   forever newly writ
          each time your eye imprints

                                        this body,
                              this text
that   will   NEVER   combúst

_____

          even after our age is done

Aut Vincere Aut Mori

They put a coin in my heart
I exchanged it for riots
Rosa Luxemburg
Leibknecht
Karl Marx —
all my cloned lapwings —
there's no money in this art
no art in money
the silver coin is the navel of the dagger
— an exchange rate for malefactors —
the crabs in red amulets like chief executives
live on land or sea
they execute their bypass with their claws
in swirled pools at my feet
this body that owns its volta
explodes downwards
— decrowns the earth —
where I found a feather at Tower Bridge :
it was the quil of Sir Walter Raleigh
I used it to spoil my ballot
to bait my spooled shoal
I had a sea-change when all horizons cleared :

the sea-change lapsed when I got to land

Subjective Knitting

in radical lace . Polemical
strapless in contentious
corset . Inflammatory
glimpse in conjugal silk .
Restive straps in purple
fishnets . Agitative susp
ension in first time red .
Pointed heels in Argento
gloss . Pinched elastic in
woven threads . Frayed
string in slippy hooks .
Obsidian stockings in
breathless gauze . Latex
belt in ribboned lengths .
Laced boots in Saxon black
. Frayed poppyhead
ripped pink to the core.

Burnt Rose

Hotel bedhangings clamped & artichoked,
lovescrawls pooled in the folds of a dress,
floodlit eyelids, Atlantic fishscales
stitched in a whorl of ash-musk,
dawnblue petals adrift down oilways, pressed relic
of Thameside flesh-sale scorched under a tree
in a park in Liverpool. Inside the pleats
a corpsed pupa de-robes a web of voiles,
bodybagged in the silk of tannins, sleeps
inside silk catacombs,
charred in the flame of a Cook's Match.

Talisman? No, burnt rose. *Forget about us.*

Teenage Riot, Daydream Nation

after the London Riots

Riot? Who would do that? Out of bricks? Dreams
would do that, out of bricks, out of skies
they have no bricks, so there are no skies, acts
of dreams, from what I dreamt to what they sd,
for they have no force, their electrics dead,
floats of milk parked (on their side) at dusk,
blue glass, tin can plumbed in white noise,
where should be force, a jack & a plug,
kiss me in shadow written on their fists.
You're cut she sd, your electrics out,
cut, cut out. But no, there is no force like the first
time's frost, you touch this echo & this loop,
when you fell the tannoy spoke
FIRE IN SHOPFRONT IN TOTTENHAM HALE
                    (wind — glass)
no bricks, no riots but acts, acts
of nights, skies made gold, flecked with bricks,
four acts, each act of words, electrics dead,
out, out — no dream is here, no dream is there.
Sez who? These are all my skies, we'll make
red dreams and recognise it with my words,
train our dreams in latticed fields, catch the skies

as over graves the taxis shone, a rank of trees

in red dreams now made of bricks
(I found, asleep, all those I loved)
(don't you see?), against the dead their bodies quick,
someone spoke in acts — acts — in mid-dreams
they had no bricks, we would give them bricks,
for their dead was wood the dead would move,
the type had set our fingers black, red light
on rain where wood was nailed, *kiss me in shadow*
                                 was all I heard.

That night the fields where riots passed,
the kids, in hoods, burned their graves,
two voices there — "skies", she sd; he sd : "acts" —
but they have no force, their electrics dead,
their floats of milks parked (on their side) at dusk,
blue glass, tin can plumbed in white noise,
red light in rain where the wood was nailed,
kiss me in shadow on their fists, the street
has moved, on each block a car torched & tarred.
And I sat there, no one asked, or asked you.
You were not there.

FIRE IN SHOPFRONT IN TOTTENHAM HALE
                  (wind — glass)
they took her & hit her in the crotch, even as
the camera turned, I heard a shout
"It's a girl, it's a fuckin girl," I knew it was her,
that (not only) was it love but I was IN love,
even as they hit her there, kicked her

in brown & blue glass, it was her I loved
— tongue, hands, feet, eyes, ears, heart —
each face that watched reflected off each face
that watched just for the fun of it. It came to pass.
Six of them came to six hot riots (Riots? Who will?
kiss me in shadow written on their fists), bent
on knees they hit as others rise, rise like zombies
cast in their own wet dream, rise & speak :
words, words, we are dreams, riots, bricks, words.

In these acts there are no skies, there are only bricks.

Man

Oh mightie love! Man is one world, and hath
another to attend him
George Herbert

Yes we accept we're centre stage
but the world has doubled in size,
the stars are map pins pressed
to the vacuum
flying back like fireflies,
I wear this tie because there's rope around my neck
but the tie is attached to the fishook of the void —
and I'm a cotton-strip of bait —
The Church tried to snuff this heresy
like a field of mechanics
chasing forest fires with black stained hands
and though I'm unionised in truth
with every other man
the opened ground beneath my feet
lures like the dressing room
of a wake-employed comedian
— the earth, the worms, the ashes —
their truth is my truth, their comfort no comfort :
each of us the adventurer, the adventuress :

a lone anaphylactic Columbus

Machines & Magazines

A dialogue between letterpress and spool
Google: "Geraldine Monk" = About 20,300 results (0.23 seconds)
The Saison Poetry Library catalogue: monk, geraldine = 38 records found
British Poetry Magazines 1914-2000: A history and bibliography of "little"
magazines: Monk, Geraldine = 7
ICA, 30 July 2009: Geraldine Monk = 1

All my life
        machines & magazines
    the switch, the swatch
lights out & something for morning
            one for the lads, one girl
        automation & process
                a console, a prize
        cardboard robots
    — machines & magazines —
        lights out, EMERGENCY CREDIT
    silver & hot pink
                creaming off the finish
        BIT soldiers
        machines & magazines
                all my life
    the standby, the chatup—
        "Princess Di might be dead but you're the Queen of my
Heart"
            the grief of the legal limit

the punchline, the enterprise
machines & magazines
the spectrum — a whizzer —
VHS ejecting its umlauts
emotions in black spools
coiling The Real
lights out
— all my life —
magazines, machines
the mush, mechanics
You pressed me wrong
a catastrophe of switches
my mind synching your silences
into the dot text FOREVER
pressed — to — magazine
compressed — in — machine

City of London Dark Hymn

On Holborn Viaduct played a game of You're so dark
you have an oilslick oyster for Old Fish Hill
past Shoe Lane You're so dark your best brogues
transfer tube dead insects
past Farringdon St You're so dark you mistook
the city rail sign for a hooked cross
past Cock Lane You're so dark your testosterone
is labelled XXX
past the sand-dust stone of the Old Bailey
You're so dark you have your own truth & reconciliation process
past Amen Court You're so dark all your blessed endings
are fresh addictions
past St Bride St You're so dark your flesh virgins
are cast forever to obsidian bronze
past Limeburner Lane You're so dark your only citrus is charred
to ash, at the carousel of Ludgate Circus
You're so dark your clowns clone tears for future downpours
down St Paul's Churchyard You're so dark you want
the cathedral's bosom realigned phallically
on Ave Maria Lane You're so dark your hymns bass thrum
to seventies porn and even in the May sun the City cloaked
its white silence was too dark to riposte

Nightwriting

By kindlelight
below the necropolis
the little grave
of Jane McCabe
died in 1825
covered with rolls
of astroturf

Our Glasnost Love

For Sarah

Back in the Häagen-Dazs we made Bang & Olufsen plans,
our mercantile enemies had Staropramen breath
— their plastic strips cashed red districts of glass —
our praline fingers melted Volkswagen buckles,
spread a flood your Scandinavian fishnets could not
hold. We let it age our Mercedes-Benz hair
more silver than a custom penknife
in the top pocket of the highest ranking M.E.P.,
his briefcase stuffed with pillowcase croissants,
anchovies shocked black your trois-fromage bloom
— *for love j'ai faim, j'ai faim for your breasts* —
our Monoprix fix axed by Teutonic crows
doppelgänging time down the strasse of our twenties,
Heloise & Abelard stumped to page more dunkel
than any Erdinger pinflaxed with onyx blackout,
down La Rambla, the slot-erotics of The Wall,
hunched for names in le pleuvoir of Père Lachaise,
all condensed — condensed for the quick — I've come
destination, this once I've arrived — your autobahn eyes.

Francis Bacon

The physiognomy of the mouth is such that rage, ecstasy and harangue are indistinguishable in appearance. Bacon's popes are shouting at least as much as they are screaming.

Andrew Brighton

Mouths blitzed snares grazing on hare's bone, mouths bruised gums rinsed red by half-bricks, mouths shrunk gasmasks descaled with calcium, mouths flaked roses scented by gaslamps, mouths wet sirens dosing on death shock, mouths helixed sphincters clamping wormed pink, mouths dead lamb's-bone flaking from shoulder, mouths frost trenchfoot dentured in nettles, mouths white slugs mangled by salt, mouths wombed navels in bombed-out structures, mouths marbled fat minced new by silence, mouths black cavities on SE1 railings, mouths boiled ox-tail served with black larvae, mouths freaked organs lactating the crucifix

Mortsafe

noun. *a heavy iron cage or grille placed over the grave of a newly deceased person during the 19th century in order to deter body snatchers.* (Dictionary.com)

Cross-hatched canoes, steel baskets weaving shadow
to stone in a crochet of emptiness.
The body lies royal beneath its portcullis.

A kind of ATM in reverse, a mortgage
taken on a chicken run you're paying off
now the body snatchers exhume your earth.

The opposite of *trough*, an OXO Puzzler
across your plated text. Fleur de lys non-existent —
DO NOT WATER or wager it will stay.

If someone had robbed a bank & hung the currency
of your appendix, the florins of your heart
— your lungs' transparencies — would have fallen

in value to keep your papers & bones in synch.
The stone of your name without your flesh
beneath : a forged cheque calcified on earth.

Every firewall has its Trojan Horse,
this the nightworm, the towncrying earwig.
No bank can crash this, no collapse, no rush,

no midnight branch run can shake the lock or latch
or crank the hinge that wagtails pick with iron wings.
When supply was in the red, Resurrectionists took you

like a sack of sourdough & all your words reduced
to this drugged zombie-look, lumbered like festive nightmail.
A shortage of deaths is a frustration for everyone.

In this world ill-supplied of murderers & lesser criminals
your blue flesh is a currency worth digging through tendrils
and worms' tendons for — the earth breaks its slag of text —

the coffin crisp as when it was laid, the final hinge
creaks like the still-to-be-fixed shed door.
You slept in sackcloth on the train; your overtime jaw

slack & green as your diggers jostled & laughed
about the trunk : a Christmas party road trip away from home.
Outside of Law, unregistered, non-documented :

your silence is dark matter in this carriage rut of stress, desire
and blackheads. Dying is decay, to live practices filth.
There were forty-nine unfinished things in your life

— boyhood dreams included — that you were going to live for.
That's been nixed : you cannot rise in a state of unfinishedness.
Call the office. Send text. Arrange a shave.

Rohypnoled, beyond London's coil
you travel dead & too late for rest.

Lungs

wheezed like a seaside squeezebox,
foot-pumped squids dashboarding the thorax.
A man on Argyle Street plays *Pop Goes the Weasel* on bagpipes,
his dying words pending the melody, hoisted on the pulmonary,
two plastic bags lift on the breeze :
Inhale, expel.
Inhale, expel.
Like heartbeats the run is finite.
Take a breath : one gone,
another : ventricles amass carbon dioxide.
She asks : *Spell Bismarck please?*
O, CK, it's CK — got it —
All words go out in the great toxin race
to flowers & trees;
the lungs, crystal kebabs, atom clouds, little Hiroshimas,
mortsafed with fabrics against the bodysnatch of the last collapsed
breath.

Fairground

Over night a colour palace, an architecture of chance in Liverpool 6,
Fairground Ltd camped on the sports pitch,
corrugates of steel bookpress the daisies
— mnemonics of first kisses —
the woman in a world of white dogs stops to breathe the sugared
tickets,

walks past the rails
as crows decimate a candy floss,
— peck the pink face of hair —
a boy pulls a father into his past
where airbrushed Disney pixelates a hawthorn,
a blackbird explodes its wings behind *Coffee & Crepes*
— a kite of sticks clatters the branches —
against an air punctuated with Ghost Train screams,

white trolleys that shunt in a shed of fake jaws
and trammel the creeping jenny that twines the tracks,
a girl in first make-up holds hands & walks like she's cut in a knife
shower —
disappears in the black-out of promised horror :

This is Anfield, this is America.

The Boy Made of Marble

For Pavel

The Boy Made of Marble leads us out
(blue veins A-road his shoulderblades)
as a crow puppetshows the floodlights,
the sun smashes the shrieking brick of the jay
— there is not time for This Little Piggy —
The warbler is a small bird with very large eyes
past a jet black burnet moth festooned with red
hearts — a Goth that does Valentines —
Dagenham Road splits apart the marsh tracks
as the Boy Made of Marble leads us left
down PUBLIC FOOTPATH No. 1
banked with shrub & gorse & ditch
a wren loonies the branches
The wren whose face is all body, body all face
— there is no time for Round & Round the Garden —
through the bark turnstile THE CHASE NATURE RESERVE
we stop, The Boy Made of Marble allows me to urinate
dry froth umbilicals the bank into The Rom
(the electric has cut out on kingfishers)
The kingfisher's New Wave made obsolete the mods
(sparrows) & rockers (starlings)
I carry The Boy Made of Marble along the bank
above nettle, barb & snag, push his wheel-machine
through the knee-length grass delirious with pollen,

we arrive in the midst of an interzone,
gingerbread estates close the woodland to a quadrant
backing us onto a row of suburban detacheds
(a far off ice-cream van jingles the sun to shreds)
a dead dormouse in the tracks like a foetal-keyring
curls inside itself, lends the earth its one good ear,
the YMCA now towering above us in white brick,
three boys & a dog crawl out from the industrial pipes
and point us back to the green gates & alley
to Rush Green Road
— there is no time for Humpty Dumpty —
the Boy Made of Marble leads us past the DANGER OF DEATH
electrics box, the pub called THE TAVERN
the pillbox bus 128 to CLAYBURY BROADWAY
the police sign FATAL COLLISION 28th MAY
the flag across The Three Travellers UNDER 'OLD' MANAGEMENT
the streets beginning to sing the heat
the kerbs ringing with happiness, the Boy looks skywards, smiling
This is a Summer arrival (annual). I love you. Now observe things.

Barry MacSweeney (1967)

Less than a grub specked in the engine's womb
less than a lock picked by the wind
less than fame — money — love
less than woodlouse
less than Rimbaud
less than health
less than gravel
less than dole
less that truth

A Bash Street Kids bouffant splits ends in a craw of consonants
a moment of no blue plaque on Charing X Road
MACSWEENEY WAS HERE
before the undertaker flanked in Soviet black
hair grey as hoarfrost bled by forged passports
took you away from the glare of your audience
in the back of a car, destination Cambridge
— via Holborn, Euston, Hampstead —
a mass crowd of stars swerving into side-doors
a dog-rug, ashtray, manual handle
— the stars numerous as the fizz of alcohol —
— the back of the undertaker's head transfixed —
bigger than Johnny Cash, Chatterton, Dylan,
his steady silent hands tapping out more than words
that motorways are just dictionaries with space inside
— CAMBRIDGE 59 MILES —

adrenalin spooring your blood's comet tails
too drunk to guess all motorways fork in silence

Headlights

like a fairground minotaur strobing towards us,
through cities, down sideroads,
coins on the dashboard sliding their credits
— locked in the head of the myth —
you, my avatar, my two-player,
our talk — always talk — on A roads, decisions to turn stations,
in the mist, or stick with the radio play of your life;
in the midnight Techpark we stopped,
you had something to talk about,
the flask of caffeine depleted,
the oiltank dial sank below zero,
rain flanked black the roads as headlights approached
sharp as hoarfrost
— the monostars of bikes —
— the doublestars of cabs —
cut by the black trunks of oaks,
the headlights swam their acres of white blossoms,
a starfield broke across scaffolds

&

You spoke : my two-player, my avatar

Orchestra

for Andy Davenport for sharing Arvo Part, LPO, RFH, 4/11/13

— the fishermen are cutting brown fish —
— and the birds feel the haul —
— they are cutting with little rods —
— cutting & catching, cutting & catching —
— the birds have eviscerated in the choir's hands —
— they have eviscerated above the fish —
— the captain's hands creel with silks —
— he winds the wire so the birds don't gut —
— he winds the wire so the fish stay caught —
— the entrails of the birds absorb in flags —
— they cut the fish to entrailed scores —
— the birds are knitted with the bones of the fish —
— he cuts the birds — guts the fish —
— to frequencies of screams the birds sleep through —
— only the captain hears the fish —
— the fish that are tied in brown bows of breathlessness —
— light guts their laminates —
— the fish are winning, refusing to eviscerate —
— they are winning, singing —
— *Come Holy Spirit, and give out*
  The heavenly radiance of your light —
— our ears' horned shells drown in waves —
— the birds beneath us, the fish above —

The Modern

1904

Rimbaud's stickleback skull
claws from a Lambeth puddle

his scales riffle hologrammatic
over Apollinaire's ID card

as if he, Guillame, could head Northbound
to Royal College Street

and X-ray his jawline for the dead kid's bones
rattling down inside his clavicle,
He walks from an Islington redbrick
checks his notebook for directions
Retour à Angel
Tube en face poste
Demander Clapham Road
4d

as if London is the metric of the mind
French poets arrive

by night-boat to Victoria
Southbound to Clapham
for fog & depression

for "great tits & a behind"

Rimbaud for a bullet's vowel
his pink cock in some milk

1918

who puts the crows in trench coats
hooded like Germans

on Grosvenor Road SW1
a pink balloon scrotums the rails

— Owen strewn maitre d' —
— Apollinaire snotted by Eros —
chaffinches arson their waistcoats,
natural gases in the bowels of a tree
— Picabia Napoleon'd in a sling —
— Céline plugs his wounds with London soot —
the fog through which
Mallarmé said
God cannot see —
O Tommy, Tommy Boys

it's 1-nil carrion
2-nil corvus

Ron King at the Estuary

Ron King walks me to the estuary & tells me of his son.
Ron King walks me to the estuary & tells me of his son's death.
Ron King walks me to the estuary & tells me of his son's death to cancer.
Ron King walks me to the estuary & tells me his son's name was Daniel.
Ron King walks me to the estuary & tells me of Daniel's death to cancer.
The bookartist Ron King tells me that his next son died (years later)
                                                    of the same cancer.
The great bookartist Ron King tells me that his son had turned to God
                                    & thought God could cure him.
The greatest bookartist of the 20th Century Ron King tells me that God
                        has punished him for his house & success.
In Ron King's book *Bluebeard's Castle* there is a room that contains
                                            a last door :
"his eye" was changed to "*the* eye" : God is in ellipsis.

The water below : a fish-tail, a white rowboat, a low-flying swallow.

On the shore of the estuary there are mounds of algae drying in the sun
like the pages of a book.

The Barry MacSweeney Guest Room

for Tim Allen & The Language Club

Wolftongue there are polar bears above my head.
Twenty-four polar bears in a scrapbook montage.
Above my head are two portraits of the Bard —
one the dot-matrix state-embossed folio shot.

After your reading did Tim drive you back via
Union Street, his homicidal sling-shot side door insecure
after the ritual elixirs of dancing liquids had done their trick
as anti-ageing remedials for the turbot-white teenagers

spewed back on a stomach surf of Kronenbourgs,
on a tide of bravado & fizz, masquerading above
the clamp of the newly pink, the fuck you flotsam
of the heart's (— as trickster, as pump —) first seaflower?

Steve & Norman in the back, I had no appetite for the diluvian
drink, the crashpad catch-up of a cold & the cache of the trains
was pushing me on for the polar bears & bards. Shit joke
at the junction : *Exit pursued by a polar bear.*

First we lost Norman through the gates of The Fin-de-Siecle
Hotel, then Steve at Khrushchev Holiday Hill. Earlier,
when we'd met at the Station, Tim had filled up on petrol
now I couldn't see the point : de-crank the handbreak

and a city of hills drops me down to the arctic sleep.
As we drove he said, Wolftongue, that you'd read
at The Language Club — Il Duce of the lexicon —
and you'd slept under the same Bard's sexless sidepart

where the white clip-on cubs flower — sweating out
the clinics with *The Book of Demons* — not stones but in the gutter —
face up to the gulls, feet down to the velveteen cactus,
as good a place as any to get yourself clean, in Tim's

upside-down house where you walk in upstairs to look
down on the birds. The peewits rang shrill but you'd
already committed to death-by-stereo. Your Gunslinger-
Dylan boots collapsed at the bed's end like chess-pieces

danced too long across disco-squares of boredom. Looking
up at the crocheted mask that once craved the selfsame froth
— apocryphally dead after a pissup with an alchemist —
you knew the peewits only wallock in flight. This mortal coil

that rings itself out in the peel of each peeled ring-pull.

My Mouth is an Elizabethan

a night hook to hang desires on, a dawndamp wench that o-blows, a ditchdog that salivates for kiosk sallets, smooths over pickedevants, shuns the rules of peccadilloes, hey ninny-ninnies the night-time hours with wounded secrets, plays naughty nuncle to a crate of Stellas, a carafe of warehouse shiraz, hurricanoes the smoke of Class Bs, perpetuates the faux mistakes bookmakers pretend to closet, smulkins magnaminous rumours, censures users of liquorice papers, angles compilation cassettes, minnikins the gargantuan for shots that can be made whole, checkouts new coinages for multipack offers, makes questrists festinate to ask for what they don't need, makes vile jellies of loose vowels & licks them like tarts, fixes facemasks of flask like whites of eggs to smooth-out accent cracks, hollas at whispers & abhors repetitions, stoples sobriety around the twilit fruit bowl, cankers after cans of Kronenbourg, stoops for Rizlas in the first light of a Girodawn, aches in the mash-up masque for the first fall-out of routine in the woodpecker's call

A Human Face

mice with wings can wear a human face
        Theodore Roethke

Swallows sail leadbolted down wires of air
— where was it, Porthmadog? — where the train stopped
and we watched them nest. That night, bats
around the woodships of the chalets
— appalled by their own interiors —
their radars the minds of subaqueous mariners.
My son laughed & broke-down laughing
— *every bat has a human face I said* —
and when a family behind us stopped to watch, he said :
every bat has a human face.